Living by Design

Your law of Attraction.

12 Principles to Live a
Healthy,
Prosperous
and Joyous Life.

Price: $12.00

© 2008 by Evaristo Lacerda

All rights reserved. No Major Part of this book may be reproduced in any form or by any electronic or mechanical means, including information storage and retrieval systems, without permission in writing. Permission will be granted upon request. The use of short quotations or occasional page copying for personal or group study is permitted and encouraged.

"Scripture taken from the New King James Version. Copyright © 1982 by Thomas Nelson, Inc. Used by permission. All rights reserved." Scriptures **"bold"** was added by the author.

Some scriptures are taken from the HOLY BIBLE, NEW INTERNATIONAL VERSION®. Copyright © 1973, 1978, 1984 International Bible Society. Used by permission of Zondervan. All rights reserved.

The "NIV" and "New International Version" trademarks are registered in the United States Patent and Trademark Office by International Bible Society. Use of either trademark requires the permission of International Bible Society.

Prologue

I was coming from church feeling that something was missing in my life. The teaching's that I had heard through the church, television and tapes had presented a mosaic of teachings; each one emphasizing some aspect of the Christian life and doctrine but never a picture of the whole truth.

Among all preachers on television I was impressed with John Oestin, Joel Oestin father. His sincerity, integrity and transparency caused me to admire and listen to him with pleasure. He had the best positive thinking message without mentioning anything about positive thinking. His teaching was coming from a highly positive view of humankind embedded in the scriptures. He could condemn sin without condemning the sinner. He taught with such candor that even the "worst" sinner would be attracted.

Every preacher finds their own way to express the gospel. There is the prophet, the healer, the positive thinker, some are inspirational other teachers of the word. Every one of them has their place in the kingdom of God. Some are eloquent orators that can use words with power and awe. There is audience for each one of them. The apostle Paul said "Certain, indeed, even through envy and contention, and certain also through good-will, do preach the Christ; the one, indeed, of rivalry the Christ do proclaim, not purely, supposing to add affliction to my bonds, and the other out of love, having known that for defense of the good news I am set; what then? in every way, whether in pretense or in truth, Christ is proclaimed -- and in this I rejoice, yea, and shall rejoice. For I have known that this shall fall out to me **for salvation,** through your supplication, and the supply of the Spirit of Christ Jesus,"(Philippians 1:15-19   Young's Literal Translation)

I taught Greek koine at the Seminary where I graduated in Theology for three years. Since then, almost 28 years ago, I have continued studying the Greek New Testament. In the above translation Paul is saying it doesn't matter the motivation for which they preached the gospel "for I have known that this shall fall out to me for salvation (of the listeners)", by prayer and the supply of the Spirit of Christ.

Of course every preacher will give account for themselves before God. But if they are preaching Christ, some people by the Holy Spirit will find salvation. That is what matters.
We are all unique in our preaching and in our hearing. Some are intellectuals. They need someone that preaches to their reason. Others are very emotional. Others are so enslaved by

addictions that only a strong word can shatter their complacency or whatever has them stagnated in life. Most of us are going through different stages of life and some teaching's can touch us in that specific stage. So every preacher has their place and time in the Kingdom.

When we find the gospel we sometimes can get "stuck" with the way we see things. Other times as we mature we feel the need for stronger nurturing. When the preacher matures with the congregation some people grow in knowledge and excitement, others stay behind and sigh about the "good old times." Even the word mature needs to be defined, where is someone "maturing" to? What direction? Maybe that is one reason why people move from church to church, looking for someone to nurture their needs.

Preachers like T.D. Jakes, Dr. Fred Price, Robert A. Schuller , Paula White, Joel Oestin, Copland, Rick Warren and an extensive parade of television personalities just in this country and hundreds of others in each country of the world, and thousands of thousands in every corner, every church, preach Sunday after Sunday the good news of Jesus Christ. Every one of them has their unique personality and their unique emphasis in some aspect of the gospel. Among them I have been impressed with Dr. Bill Winston teaching's.

When I listened to the series "The Renewing of Your Mind", it was so striking that it caused me to rethink and rewrite all my theology. I find myself in the place of my life where I can see all pieces of knowledge coming together in a wonderful symphony.

I was 17 years old when I came to the knowledge of Christ as my Savior. At that time I started listening and appreciating classical music. We had a lady in the church teaching us how to sing the chorus following the notes, solfege (the application of the sol-fa syllables to a musical scale or to a melody) etc. Then I bought the partiture (sheet music) of Beethoven's Moonlight Sonata, I didn't know what "for the 8th year" meant, so I started "wood pecking" the song. One day by one those divine appointment I heard someone playing a beautiful, wonderful, melodious song. To my dismay there was a young lady practicing in the church on the grand piano for her recital that night no other song than the Moonlight Sonata. After that the little parts that I was trying to play came together in a wonderful symphony.

This book is about this great symphony of life when all instruments come together in harmony. Thank you Pastor Bill. Now I see the creation with a clear purpose. Life was meant to be abundant, prosperity as the fruit of righteousness, blessed to be a blessing, the dominion of the earth, walking by faith, the transfer of riches, heaven on earth, the power of visualization and confession, the work of the subconscious mind and so many other aspects of the Kingdom of God among us.

Mr. Miles Monroe is part of this better understanding of the implications of living the Kingdom here and now.

All came together. My wife Nancy and I took a weekend in a hotel away from everybody just to listen to all the tapes and meditate on the meaning of Romans 12:2

"Do not conform any longer to the pattern of this world, but be transformed by the renewing of your mind. Then you will be able to test and approve what God's will is —his good, pleasing and perfect will" (NIV)

This book is about the revelation of a new view of life, an explosive view of what walking by faith and walking in health, abundance and joy really means. It all starts in our mind. After reading the principles exposed in this book and letting them sink into the subconscious mind, we will understand what is meant by "Welcome to the Kingdom of Heaven."

Acknowledgments

To my Wife Nancy C. Lacerda
   and our daughters :
   Jamie , Rachel, Lea ,Debora and Ester.

   My brother: J. Rodolfo Schaffer (Rudi), and to our mother Apolinesia, who started it all.

   Our Living by Design LoA Group.

   And Kattie Lata, Pat Aldridge, Susan Markham and Sherry A. Sharpe for the improvements in the originals.

"Happiness is to be in the center
   of God's Perfect Will"
αγαθον και ευαρεστον και τελειον

Good, Pleasant and Perfect Rm. 12:2

            To the King of kings and Lord of lords
               to Him that reign forever
           Be all the Glory, Praise and Thanksgiving

Table of Contents

Prologue	3
Introduction	10
First Principle "We Are What We Think The Most"	17
Second Principle. "Guide your Thoughts"	23
Third Principle. "Emotion Guidance System"	27
Fourth Principle. " Born to Enjoy Life"	30
Fifth Principle. "Our Inner Man"	33
Sixth Principle. " Believe you Have Received"	40
Seventh Principle. "Allowing Time"	44
Eighth Principle. " Visualization "	49
Ninth Principle. " Confession "	53
Tenth Principle. " A New Way of Thinking"	56
Eleventh Principle. " There is Enough for Everyone"	60
Twelfth Principle. " Be an Uplifter "	66
Epilogue.	71
Biography	76
Bibliography	79

Introduction

"Know that all things work together for good to them that love God, to them who are the called according to his purpose." Romans 8:28

God is good, all the time.

"Give thanks to the LORD, for he is good; His love endures forever." Psalm 118

Living by Design your Law of Attraction. We say that the universe was created by design. The human kind was created for greatness, to live a healthy, prosperous and happy life. When someone do not understand that they create their own point-of-view of life. Some people say life is hard and to them life is very hard, others say life is a mystery and they wander through life, others say "well life is just life", so life is just "wherever". There is an interesting interaction between our attitude about life and our circumstances. We may influence our circumstances through our attitudes or we may be influenced by the circumstance according to our view of life. If everything is going smoothly, we tend to say life is beautiful.

When things change and become harsh we tend to complain and see life as not so wonderful. What we hear and what we experience create in us a perception of the world, of life itself, influencing our interpretation of the circumstances around us. The way you see life will determine your level of happiness. So, what is life? How should we see it?

The Bible says life is good, always.

God created the universe with love. He created you and I with one desire in His Mind, one purpose; To enjoy life in Him.

He wants to save all mankind. "God our Saviour, who desires all men to be saved and to come to the knowledge of the truth." (I Timothy 2:4) More than creating us to Worship Him, (and we do it in gratitude), or being created to have dominion over the earth, and we do with Him, He had in mind to duplicate Himself in happy creatures as He is a happy God. We read in I Timothy 1:11 "the glorious gospel of the blessed God" the word "blessed" here is from the greek "μακαριου" the same used in Acts 26:2 "I think myself happy".

God by definition is all sufficient. He doesn't "need" someone else to complete Him. In His completeness He is blessed and in creating mankind He extended in us His happiness, His love. He has good pleasure in creating us "to enjoy Him" (John Piper)

"**In love** He predestined us to be adopted as His sons through Jesus Christ, in accordance with His **pleasure and will**— to the praise of His **glorious grace**, which He has **freely given us** in the One He loves. In him we have redemption through his blood, the forgiveness of sins, in accordance with the **riches of God's grace** that He **lavished on us** with all wisdom and understanding. And He made known to us the mystery of His will according to **His good pleasure**, which He purposed in Christ, to be put into effect when the times will have reached their fulfillment—to bring all things in heaven and on earth together under one head, even Christ."(Ephesians 1:5-10)

With love and good pleasure He created and "predestined" us. Predestined is to set the limitations. I make a hammer for "hammering" things. If I try to "wash dishes" with a hammer I will make a mess. Man was destined to "walk with God in happiness", when he tries to use his life for something else he only fools himself.

"So God created man in His own image...God saw all that He had made, and it was **very good** " (Genesis 1:31)

He created a paradise for His sons to live in.

"Now the LORD God had planted a **garden** in the east, in Eden;

and there He put the man He had formed. And the LORD God made all kinds of trees grow out of the ground—trees that were **pleasing to the eye and good for food.** " (Genesis 2:6)

Paradise on earth was the temporary place made in the image of the one that would be permanent. The New Earth, the paradise for ever. The things that we see now are "shadows of the things to come" (Colossians 2:17). The Garden or the paradise on earth was made according to the image of the one eternal.

About this paradise we read:

To the repented thief on the cross Jesus told him, "I tell you the truth, today you will be with me in **paradise**." (Luke 23:43).

The Apostle Paul had an extraordinary experience, he said: "I know a man who...was caught up to **paradise**. He heard inexpressible things, things that man is not permitted to tell." (2 Corinthians 12:4)

And in the book of Revelation John is told: "To him who overcomes, I will give the right to eat from the tree of life, which is in the **paradise** of God. " (Revelation 2:7)

Christ is the door to this paradise. Through Him Heaven

comes to earth, through Him earth goes to Heaven, to a New Heaven and New Earth, paradise is restored.

We have been made to live in paradise but sin has distorted the image of God in us and has prevented us to enter such a place but, Thank God, through repentance and the renewing of our mind we are born again and introduced into His Kingdom. We are born into the family of God. From creatures we become Sons of the Almighty.

"Yet to all who received him, to those who believed in His name, he gave the right to become children of God—children born not of natural descent, nor of human decision or a husband's will, but born of God. " (John 1:12, 13)

Now in Christ we are called to live what God had intended for us, Abundant Life.

"I came that they may have and enjoy life, and have it in abundance (to the full, till it overflows). (John 10:10 AMP). Abundant, Greek περισσον, perisson. Definition: exceeding some number or measure or rank or need over and above, more than is necessary, super added, exceeding abundantly, supremely, something further, more, much more than all, more plainly. One word may summarize: overflow.

That is the life God wants you to have, but this life does not come just with conversion. Conversion or "new birth" is the turning point. We are exposed to a new way of living, now we need to take possession of this life. Newborns are like a baby, they need food to grow.

"As newborn babes, desire the pure milk of the word, that you may grow thereby" (I Peter 2:1)

The primary food is the Word of God. The Bible is like a university. We start in kindergarten and then we are stimulated to grow in the knowledge of His Word "that is able to build us up." (Acts 20:32)

"For this reason, since the day we heard about you, we have not stopped **praying for you** and asking God to fill you with the **knowledge of His will** through all spiritual wisdom and understanding. And you pray this in order that you may live a life worthy of the Lord and may please him in every way: bearing fruit in every good work, **growing in the knowledge of God,** being strengthened with all power according to His glorious might so that you may have great endurance and patience, and **joyfully giving thanks** to the Father, who has qualified you to **share in the inheritance** of the saints in the **kingdom of light**. For He has rescued us from the dominion of darkness and brought us into the **kingdom of the Son** he loves, in whom we have redemption, the forgiveness of sins" (Colossians 1.9-14)

"Therefore let us leave the elementary teachings about Christ and go on to maturity, not laying again the foundation of repentance from acts that lead to death..." (Hebrews 6:1)

To grow in knowledge of God we can use tools that enhance our understanding of His Word, like Geography, History, languages etc. The apostle Paul read different books and advised us that we should,

"Test all things; hold fast what is good." (I Thessalonians 5:21)

Through reading books about the mind and the laws that govern success we find many principles that have been created by God for our good. Principles that have been in His Word written thousands of years ago and in the human mind since the creation.

I want to review some principles that are in line with God's teachings for our lives.

Here are 12 easy principles that when understood, will enhance our lives and enable us to live to the full potential that God intended.

Chapter 1
First Principle

We are what we think the most

Every successful person in this world will say that they had something that drove them to the place where they are now. When we read their biographies, we can identify that there was a dominant thought that brought circumstances, events or people in the direction they had in mind. From this finding we derive the first principle of the law of attraction: Our dominant thoughts bring about actions, events and circumstances.

Whatever we think, negative or positive, this continuous thought will bring negative or positive results in our life. The bible tells us the story-drama of a man that, although he was a good man, because he harbored a wrong thought in his mind, he brought disastrous results to himself. We read the drama of Job.

"There was a man in the land of Uz, whose name was Job; and that man was blameless and upright, and one who feared God and shunned evil". (Job 1:1)

But, although he was a good man, one day he lost everything he had. His friends could not understand how in this world this good man could lose family, goods, everything. For the most part of the book his friends try to find one fault in him that could explain the reason of his suffering. But he, himself, gave us the reason of his "misfortune".

"...the thing I greatly feared has come upon me, And what I dreaded has happened to me." (Job 3:25)

Every time his sons and daughters had a party, a feast in their home, he immediately ran to offer sacrifices because he thought; they could have done something wrong. His fear that something bad could happen to them broke the fence he had around him and brought what he feared the most. His dominant thought operated in his life. In the book of Proverbs we read:

"For as he thinks in his heart, so is he." (Proverbs 23:7)

Our thinking has a tremendous power that most of the time we don't consider. Lynne McTaggart in the book "The Field" writes; "We live in a zero-field ocean of energy where subatomic particles move, coming into and disappearing of existence." Quantum science has been marveled about this phenomenon in the subatomic level. The "space" between atoms and electrons is composed of vibrating energy where all things move.

Reading the Greek philosophers of his time, the apostle Paul in Athens quoted.

"for in Him we live and move and have our being, as also some of your **own poets** have said, 'For we are also His offspring.' Therefore, since we are the offspring of God, we ought not to think that the Divine Nature is like gold or silver ..."(Acts 17:28,29)

The poets or philosophers, one of them probably Plato, who wrote in "timeus" that God through demiurgos created the humankind. Paul goes along with the line that God created man, mankind are offspring from God. And Paul, by the Holy Spirit, adds mankind lives in God. "... in Him we live, we move and have our being"

Unfortunately, sin operates like a shield around every person separating them from God, they move in God, but they can't reach him although He is so near. Sin separates man from God. But through repentance, coming to the truth, the truth sets us free, and then the wall of separation is broken. Now in Christ we can truly "live, move and have our being" in God, we can have communion with Him. We can pray anywhere, anytime. We are in Him.

That is why it doesn't matter where we are, God is there, because we move in the spiritual realm, we move in Him.

It is in this ocean of invisible subatomic particles/waves, created by God and an extension of God that we and the whole universe live. This ocean of energy is the medium where waves of electricity, magnet or sounds move in. In this ocean our minds are sending out waves. Each thought is not just the passage of chemical/electrical signals between neurons but the emission of frequencies. Looking at an EEG, the electroencephalogram is the device that registers the electrical waves that come from our mind; we see how many frequencies are going out of our mind at any given time. Those waves go throughout the universe and can resonate with similar frequencies creating harmony or disharmony, bringing results that are still a vast science field that we are just tapping into.

How many times we are near someone and they start humming or whistling a song that we were just thinking about. Or in a conversation someone raises a subject we were just thinking about. Telepathy is still a young science. But it is not too long before the day comes when we may turn on or off lamps, radios etc., or even have devices that enhance the right waves and we will communicate thought to thought. In March 2008, Texas Instruments demonstrated a device that could be worn in the neck and could read the waves sent to our vocal chords and with the help of a computer it transform signals into commands for a wheel chair. Without a voice someone was giving commands to the wheel chair, where to go where to turn and when to stop.

The mind is a powerful device with tremendous energy that we need to guide in the best direction. What we think will affect our lives, it doesn't matter if we believe in this law or not. Our dominant thoughts will bring about emotions, people, events, and circumstances.

Every time we have a dominant thought we are sending out a tremendous amount of energy that is exercising control over our body, that is affecting people and circumstances around us. In Romans 4 verse 17 Paul says: "God, who gives life to the dead and calls those things which do not exist as though they did;" By words God brought from nihil, nothingness, and the cosmos.

You influence your body by your thoughts. After a nightmare you may wake up sweating and your heart maybe beating faster. Your mind is creating your universe. You have the power to design your destiny. It all starts in your thinking.

Chapter 2
Second Principle:

We must guide our thoughts to achieve the best outcome

The Bible says: "casting down arguments and every high thing that exalts itself against the knowledge of God, **bringing every thought into captivity to the obedience of Christ**,"(2 Corinthians 10:5)

The word "captivity" in the Greek text is used for "going to the enemy's camp, sizing them and bringing them captive". In every thought that comes to my mind I have the power and duty to analyze it to determine if they are convenient or not, if this thought is good or a waste of time, or worse, can this thought drive me down to harmful things. I must capture it and bring it under obedience to the good things God wants in my life.

Many people think they are guided or misguided by their emotions. We heard about "crime of passion", the ones committed under an uncontrollable emotion. We understand that emotions are powerful, but emotions are caused by thoughts, when we let one thought come in and we nurture that thought it will cause emotions and then by continuing that thought we empower the emotion to the point that the emotion grows disproportionately and begins to "control" us. The first thing we need to do is not to invite or not to let uninvited thoughts dwell in our minds. We control our thoughts and we direct them to where we want to go.

We read about Cain how he was misguided by a strong emotion against his brother, and ended up killing him. Let's see the steps he went through. God had established a way to do the sacrifices. When Adam and Eve committed the disobedience, they should physically die. The order of God was "you must not eat from the tree of the knowledge of good and evil, for when you eat of it **you will surely die."** (Gen 2:17 NKJV). They knew they would die someday, that's why they had the tree of life in the garden, but sin would cut off their time of living in the earth. But when they ate from the tree of knowledge they didn't die, at least physically. God provided someone else to die for them. "The LORD God made garments **of skin** for Adam and his wife and clothed them." (Gen 3:21. NKJV) Something had to die to have it's skin covering the couple, that was a type of Christ dying for our sins, and God was establishing the sacrifices of animals as a way for man to think before doing wrong. Cain knew it, but he decided to offer something else. His brother did the right thing; he came from the altar with peace in his heart. Cain didn't feel good because he didn't do the right thing. Now that feeling of not being accepted started growing in him and he started looking to his brother as the culprit for his "inability of being accepted" and he let those emotions grow against his brother. But God looking at Cain's heart still came to him and says:

"Why are you angry? Why is your face downcast? If you do what is right, will you not be accepted? But if you do not do what is right, sin is crouching at your door; it desires to have you, **but you must master it**." (Gen 4:6,7)

God is good all the time.

Even when Cain had done the wrong thing, God still came to him and gave him an opportunity to think about and do the right thing. "Sin is at your door, but you must master it". He could go back and present the right offering but instead he went on and killed his brother.

Some people reading this account come with an interesting question. Why didn't God deliver Abel?

God gave the dominion of the earth to man: "Then God said, "Let Us make man in Our image, according to Our likeness; let them have dominion..." (Gen 1:26) Once God gave you the dominion of the earth, now it is up to you to decide what you want to do. We don't know what Abel had in his mind but he saw his brother bring to the altar what he was not supposed to. He saw his countenance downcast, which should be enough for him to get away. The counsel of God is "Make no friendship with an **angry man**, and with a furious **man** do not go," (Prov. 22:24). Abel didn't take dominion of his life driving himself away from an irate man. Thinking by default, meaning not taken proper action, he fell a victim of "circumstance".

Yes God can intervene, He is Sovereign but most of time He lets the laws He created work on their own so we can understand that we need to exercise dominion. We must understand all His natural laws and use them for our good. We must have dominion over our thought life. To do good and get away from evil.

Your dominant thoughts will bring circumstances, so you better direct your thoughts to the things, emotions and outcome that you want. Thinking by default is when we do not focus on the things we want. Then our mind wanders from here to there, without any objective, we are living adrift. When people say: "I don't care, whatever happens, just happens", they are thinking by default, and default is dangerous. You don't have to think hard or monitor your thoughts all the time. There is an easy way to keep your thoughts in the right direction. Our Emotional Guide System.

Chapter 3
Third Principle

Our Emotions tell us if we are going in the right direction

The best way to know that we are thinking right is when we feel peace inside of ourselves, peace with God. That is one of the reasons we must choose joyful thoughts; be thankful for the things we have and for the good things that are coming. It is very important, it is crucial to keep our mind focused on joyful thoughts, because thoughts bring emotions. Negative emotions such as sadness, anger, jealousy, depression, etc. are the result of something we were thinking. We need to go back to the source of that thought and make a decision. If there is something that we need to do now, we need to take action, but if the feeling is because of wrong thinking, we must change the line of our thoughts immediately.

We need to meditate always on good things. "Finally, brethren, whatever things are true, whatever things are noble, whatever things are just, whatever things are pure, whatever things are lovely, whatever things are of good report, if there is any virtue and if there is anything praiseworthy—meditate on these things."(Philippians 4:8.)

Let us memorize: Whatever is True, Noble, Just, Pure, Lovely, of Good Report, Virtue, and Praiseworthy meditate on these things. The beautiful thing about our mind is that we tend to get use to the things we think the most.

So, let us think about edification, our edification and everybody else's edification. "Let no corrupt word proceed out of your mouth, but what is good for necessary edification, that it may impart grace to the hearers." (Ephesians 4:29).

One way to reach a life full of joy and contentment is to be thankful for the many things we have received; we need to count our blessings. When people look and talk about lack, they are attracting more lack. Think about abundance of joy, abundance of provision. God is faithful. He rewards the thoughts of our mind. That's why "in everything give thanks; for this is the will of God in Christ Jesus for you." (1 Thessalonians 5:18). In everything, give thanks. And: "Rejoice in the Lord always. Again I say, rejoice! Let your gentleness be known to all men. The Lord is at hand. Be anxious for nothing, but in everything by prayer and supplication, **with thanksgiving,** let your requests be made known to God; and the peace of God, which surpasses all understanding, will guard your hearts and minds through Christ Jesus."(Philippians 4:4-7)

If you say to yourself, be anxious for nothing, and repeat that again and again, that shows that you are anxious. What you are trying to avoid is what you are thinking the most. The more you think the more you attract it, thus The Law of Attraction. Paul is saying, if you "feel" anxious... feeling is the result of thoughts, you are not putting your trust in the provision of God and you are not exercising faith. Change your thought immediately, go to God in prayer and meditation with thanksgiving... the key of a joyful life. Thanksgiving. If we have a son that is constantly complaining that he does not have this or that, and never acknowledge the things he already has, how do we feel? Likewise our heavenly Father has given us so much, we need to acknowledge and be thankful for whatever we have, and in doing this we are making room for more in our lives.

We do not need to monitor our thoughts. We just need to watch our feelings. When we feel something different from joy, we need to look at the thoughts that brought us those feelings and take the appropriate action. Think about happiness because that is the reason we are born. This is our next principle.

CHAPTER 4
The Fourth Principle

We are born to enjoy life.

"I have come that you may have life and life in abundance" (John 10:10)

We read in Genesis 1:31 "God saw all that He had made, and it was very good". If you read the whole first chapter of Genesis you will see at least 5 times, "God saw, it was good" in Hebrew, va'iar Elohim, ki tov. And saw God, that's good!!!, and in the last verse we read: He saw it was tov m(e)'od, very good. That tells me the sense of joy God had when He finished the creation, including the human kind. It was Very Good.

Creation is good, mankind is good. Verse 27 "So God created man in his own image... 28, God blessed them" God is love and justice. We see inside of us this sense of love and justice. We rage when we see injustice, but we feel mercy when someone is in need. That is the God image inside of us. God is a good God, full of contentment, joy, and happiness. He created the humankind in His image to be happy and full of contentment.

We see this happiness in the natural world. Have you seen how our pets show happiness? How they are playful? Puppies chase one another, hide, run, bark and wag their tails to show how "happy" they are. Is it not the same with babies? Of course not barking or wagging...but we still have games in our adult life that resemble our toys and moods of infancy. Happiness is inside all of us.

We are born with happiness, that's why we pursue happiness because we want more of it. We just need to remember that happiness is inside of us, not outside, somewhere else, depending on people or circumstances. Enjoy the coffee in the morning, the bright sun, the place where we live, the people around us. We must show our young children that happiness is inside of us. We enjoy thoughts of peace, love and gladness, and through our thoughts we bring good circumstances. Our joy is not because of the circumstances but because of the thoughts that brought them.

I read about a man that went through the concentration camp without loosing his mind. He kept saying to himself that they could take everything from him but not his thoughts.

The happiness of my thoughts bring happy circumstances, and even when circumstances are not the most desirable I still think about good things and I know things will turn around. If I follow my Inner Man the image of God inside me, everything is going to be alright. We are created to enjoy what we do when we do the things that we are created for. Our assignment is our passion, our passion is our assignment. If we are not happy in what we are doing, we need to rediscover what our passion is and serve others with the things that we are passionate about, here we find our assignment in life. Paul said to Timothy in the second epistle chapter 1 verse 6 "Therefore I remind you to stir up the gift of God which is in you ". What gift is in you? Are you happy with your life?

I Read a book about "Do What You Love and Money Will Follow". We are created for happiness, to an abundant life, to be blessed in order to be a blessing. All these things start in our mind and in researching our soul, discovering who we really are.

.

Chapter 5
The Fifth Principle

Our Inner Being Is Immanently Good

The prayer of Paul to the early Christian was "that He would grant you, according to the riches of His glory, to be strengthened with might through His Spirit in the **inner man** "(Ephesians 3:16).

Our inner man is our soul, our spiritual side, the real "us". It is said today that soul and body are one and the same thing, that we are energy and our soul is our mind, our thoughts. The Bible says our body is the temple of the Spirit. God created man from the dust and then He breathed His Spirit, His breath and man was made "nephesh", soul.

Our soul is part of God in us. "Then God said, "Let us make man in Our image, according to Our likeness;", "Then God saw everything that He had made, and indeed it was very good", "And the LORD God formed man of the dust of the ground, and breathed into his nostrils the breath of life; and man became a living being." (Genesis 1:26,31 and 2:7).

God breathed on man, this is our likeness to God, His breath on us. The knowledge of good and bad was at the reach of the hand. Man was innocent, his soul and mind were working together, what he was learning was in agreement with his good inner soul. There was peace, joy, harmony. But mankind was created to make decisions, and unfortunately they can make bad decisions too. Sin distorted the image of God in us. But thank God today in Christ we can be made one again. "For he himself is our peace, who has made the two one and has destroyed the barrier, the dividing wall of hostility, by abolishing in his flesh the law with its commandments and regulations". His purpose was to create in himself one new man out of the two, thus making peace, and in this one body to reconcile both of them to God through the cross, by which he put to death their hostility. He came and preached peace to you who were far away and peace to those who were near. For through him we both have access to the Father by one Spirit. "(Ephesians 2:14-18)

We have peace inside because we have been reconciled with God; we are in harmony, mind and soul. "Therefore, if anyone is in Christ, he is a new creation; the old has gone, the new has come! All this is from God, who reconciled us to himself through Christ and gave us the ministry of reconciliation: that

God was reconciling the world to himself in Christ, not counting men's sins against them. And he has committed to us the message of reconciliation."(II Corinthians 5:17-19).

Our soul now is in contact with God, reconciled. That is our spiritual life; the spiritual side that died in the garden after the couple disobeyed God and reached out to the tree of the knowledge of good and evil. Our mind still receives all kinds of thoughts but now we can discern what is good or not, what is in harmony with God and our Inner Soul.

Before the knowledge of Christ we were "...dead in your transgressions and sins, in which you used to live when you followed the ways of this world and of the ruler of the kingdom of the air, the spirit who is now at work in those who are disobedient. All of us also lived among them at one time, gratifying the cravings of our sinful nature and following its desires and thoughts." (Ephesians 2:1-3).

Every child is born in innocence. "Jesus said, "Let the little **children come** to **me**, and do not hinder them, for the kingdom of heaven belongs to such as these." (Matthew 19:14) As with Adam there will be the time of reason, when they reach the age of making conscious decisions. Then the sinful nature kicks in, they do what their ancestors handed down to them. "For you know that it was not with perishable things such as silver or gold that you were redeemed from the empty way of life handed down to you from your forefathers,"(I Peter 1:18)

Through Christ our sinful nature is crucified with Him in the cross. "Those who belong to Christ Jesus **have crucified** the sinful nature with its passions and desires" (Galatians 5:24 NIV)

The sinful nature, the dominant principle to humankind is taken away in the cross. Although we still have to decide what thoughts will dwell in our minds, we now are not subject to sin anymore. We are called to master it, to live in the other side of the equation. "For **sin** shall not have **dominion** over you, for you are not under law but under grace."(Romans 6:14).

We are called to live under the spiritual life, in peace with our Inner Being, our soul. "**Walk** in the **Spirit**, and you shall not fulfill the lust of the flesh." (Galatians 5:16).
"There is therefore now no condemnation to those who are in Christ Jesus, who do not **walk** according to the flesh, but according to the **Spirit**." (Romans 8:1).

The flesh, in the sense of bad desires, is our old nature. It has been crucified, the old "me" with the old way of thinking. The new "me" now is invited to live in newness of life and must not let the old "me" come back, because it is dead. The Bible says "**Mortify** therefore your members which are upon the earth; fornication, uncleanness, inordinate affection, evil concupiscence, and covetousness, which is idolatry." (Colossians 3:5). Mortify is to put to death. Every time I see in me an old way of thinking I need to put it to death. The more we focus in the new way, the more the old "me" stays in the past.

Another way in which we see the consequence of the law of the mind is what I try to push away stays with me longer, because I am thinking about it. I am giving energy to that idea. I am energizing the idea that I am trying to push back. What we resist persists. Now to "mortify" it is to declare it dead, leave it there and concentrate in the new. Focus on the good things and the old "me" goes away.

Do not give harbor to evil thoughts. "take up the shield of faith, with which you can extinguish all the flaming arrows of the evil one." (Ephesians 6:16) Flaming arrows are malevolent thoughts that are thrown into our mind, we may let them intrude and stay in our thoughts or we can extinguish them with the shield of trust and faith.

Our Inner Being is good, in Christ we are a new creation, we have new life, and we need to walk in this spirit, in peace with God and with ourselves, in harmonious thoughts and soul. When we feel depression, rage, anguish, anxiety, or any negative emotion it is because our thoughts are not in line with our soul. Let us walk in the spirit "So I say, walk by the Spirit, and you will not gratify the desires of the sinful nature". For the sinful nature desires what is contrary to the Spirit, and the Spirit is contrary to the sinful nature. They are in conflict with each other, so that you are not to do whatever you want. But if you are led by the Spirit, you are not under the law (of the old nature). The acts of the sinful nature are obvious: sexual immorality, impurity and debauchery; idolatry and witchcraft; hatred, discord, jealousy, fits of rage, selfish ambition, dissensions, factions and envy; drunkenness, orgies, and the like. I warn you, as I did before, that those who live like this will not inherit the kingdom of God. "But the **fruit of the Spirit is love, joy, peace, patience, kindness, goodness, faithfulness, gentleness and self-control**. Against such things there is no law. Those who belong to Christ Jesus have crucified the sinful nature with its passions and desires. Since we live by the Spirit, let us keep in step with the Spirit. "(Galatians 5:16-25 NIV)

Walking in a negative mood or in abundance is a daily decision that becomes a habit. The old nature died on the cross with Christ, but the evil one will try to bring old habits and thoughts to disturb our inner peace, our communion with God. The renewing of the mind is to rid our mind of the old habits; the shield of faith is our trust in the Almighty that we can live in total harmony, in peace and joy.

Let your spirit guide you, always. Your soul has been sealed, and received the impartation of the Holy Spirit, "and no one can say, "Jesus is **Lord**," except by the Holy **Spirit**." (I Corinthians. 12:3). The Holy Spirit has convinced you, baptized you in the body of Christ, introduced you in the kingdom of heaven, He has broken the wall of separation between you and God, and He has restored your communication with the Father. Your soul now has a spiritual life that was dead before the new birth. Now you are invited to walk in a new life "Therefore we were buried with Him through baptism into death, that just as Christ was raised from the dead by the glory of the Father, even so we also should walk in **newness** of life. But now we have been delivered from the law, having died to what we were held by, so that we should serve in the **newness** of the Spirit and not in the oldness of the letter. " (Romans 6:4 and 7:6)

Follow your inner man, your spiritual soul, walk in newness of life, in abundance of love, peace and joy. Walk in confidence that God cares about you; He has provision for whatever you need. That is our next principle. Ask and will be given to you.

Chapter 6
The Sixth Principle

Believe that you have received the things you ask for.

"Therefore I tell you, whatever you ask for in prayer, **believe** that you have **received** it, and it will be yours." (Mark 11:24). We can look at many translations of this verse, but the Greek has no variation on the past tense of receive. The Greek word "ελαβετε" elabete, is the past tense. Christ said, Ask, the Greek word aiteo, means to request or even demand, believing that you have already received, and then it will be (future) yours. There is a buffer of time between the asking and receiving. But during this time, you have the image in your mind that you have already received. The manifestation of what you requested can take seconds or years. You have the image that it is already yours, without a doubt. Doubt is negative, belief is positive. You ask, you believe, you hold the image of already having, leave the image there, enjoy the thing you asked for, and then, voilà it will manifest in due time.

The time between asking and its manifestation depends on two things. Is your mind in agreement with your soul? You may ask something that is not good for you in the long range. "You ask and do not receive, because you ask amiss, that you may spend it on your pleasures." (James 4:3). Your Inner Being, your soul restored in communion with the Spirit, wants the best for you, and sometimes you are asking for something that will harm you. Then you may wonder why it is taking so long to manifest the thing that you ask for? The buffer of time is a time to clarify if what you want is really in alignment with your Inner being.

The second thing to receiving the manifestation of what you asked for is to believe. Will it be good for you and do you really believe? "But let him ask in faith, with no doubting, for he who doubts is like a wave of the sea driven and tossed by the wind. For let not that man suppose that he will receive anything from the Lord; he is a double-minded man, unstable in all his ways "(James 1:6-8)

Interesting is the word believe in the Bible is pisteuo, from the root peitho, meaning I persuade myself, I am persuaded. To believe is to be persuaded about something. This persuasion comes from facts or things that happen in the past and I am persuaded, convinced it will happen again. It is not a wish, but a conviction. When I say I believe it means, I am entirely convinced, persuaded, sure that it will happen because it has happened before or because it is a law and the law follows its way.

Here you are and your bank account is down, just a little bit or nothing. You ask in prayer that you want to have $10,000 in your account. It is for your good, you want to be able to help someone in need, to invest in your career, whatever is good for you and people around you. Now you believe you have received. You keep the image of that $10,000 in your account. You may open the account, if you don't have one yet. You may put 20 dollars a week or 100 dollars a month. You are just enjoying the thought of having that $10,000 dollars there. Suddenly someone asks you to do something and in exchange they gave you $500, or out of the blue came $8,000 unexpected. Just by believing, the laws in your mind are working for you. Not because you believe in the "law of attraction", but because you believe that God has created laws in the universe to bring good things to the ones that love Him. We believe God is a good God, and He wants you to prosper if you have the right thought in your mind.

If you believe that you should not be prosperous, that riches are filthy, that rich people are a disgrace to this world, then, your will be done. You are what you think about. If you think, well I wish I had that $10,000 then you do not believe, you are not persuaded, and it will not manifest. If you think "why is it taking so long?" Then you are concentrating on the lack of it, why "is it not" there yet? Concentrating on the lack, will bring more lack. All these are negative thoughts. **What you resist persists**.

Stay in the positive; believe that you have already received. Enjoy that thought, work for it without thinking about how or when it is going to happen, let the God of all provision move the universe in your favor.

I just listened about this man that was making $11.00 an hour in a mill and retired with $3,000,000 dollars in his account. He gave $2,000,000 to the local school and hospital. There are thousands of people that reached a better place in life; they discovered "the secret". They are a living proof that what you have in your mind that is what you get.

Unfortunately many people do not believe they can accomplish something. For them it looks impossible. But you are here, reading, meditating, and incorporating those principles in your life. You know that you can because you believe. So ask, believing and enjoy what you are going to receive as if you have already received and allow time for the manifestation. This is our next principle.

Chapter 7
The Seventh Principle

Allowing time between the thought and its manifestation

The seed is a good example how thoughts grow and manifest in the physical world. We must plant good thoughts to have a good harvest. " Now may He who supplies seed to the sower, and bread for food, supply and multiply the seed you have sown and increase the fruits of your righteousness," (2 Corinthians 9:10).

Thoughts are seeds that at the proper time will bloom, and bring fruits. "And let us not grow weary while doing good, for in due season we shall reap if we do not lose heart." (Galatians 6:9). In due time means that your laws of attraction work on their own. If you have a thought about something but you are not sure if you should have it or not, it is like a seed in a dry land and it may never manifest. You may see a thought manifest more quickly depending on the belief you have and you show your belief by the joy you have in thinking about what you have asked for. Time is accelerated by joyful thoughts: "Until now you have asked nothing in My name. Ask, and you will receive, that your **joy** may be full." (John

16:24).

Ask for more joy in your life, more health, and more wealth. Ask believing, and let the thought of having it be in your mind in joy. If any thought of doubt comes, do not fight against the thought of doubt, just re-focus on the thing you want and rejoice in receiving it. In due time, it will manifest on its own so your joy will be full and complete.

How do I reach what I want quicker? Sometimes we think of ways to reach what we want, but it is very important that we choose paths that bring joy. You want to have a credit card paid in the next 5 months, and you think about getting a second job but you hate the idea of working more hours outside home. This is not the best way to reach what you have asked for. Hating the job will not let you enjoy the thought of having the bill paid. The question is what can I do that I enjoy in order to get what I asked for?

In any situation in life, it could be to make a career change, or reach higher goals, but always do this through a joyous path. I read a book about doing what you like and money follows. I have seen this in my personal life and family. My daughters, early in life decided what they wanted to be. One started playing the guitar at 5 years old. I was teaching the basics to a group in our church and she was just watching, after the class she got the guitar and start putting her fingers in D plus position. I asked who had taught her and she just said "I saw you doing it", then I showed her how to do the other two chords. In two weeks we had a service in the local school, guess who played the guitar? Of course we sang slowly to give her time to change the chords, it was a memorable date. At 9 she decided to go to the conservatory and learn piano. I never had to ask her to go nor if she had done her home work. She just loved it. She finished the conservatory and some years later she started giving classes at home, at that time she wasn't making enough money. She decided to find a job somewhere else then she was not happy with the job. She decided to go back to music and applied for a school where she was hired as a choir director. She became the supervisor, but she was not happy supervising chorus. She quit and went back to choir director and then she decided to learn to sing opera. Finally she applied for singing in the Philharmonic Choral and Orchestra of Sao Paulo State. And that is what she does now, singing from her soul, "happy as a lark in the meadow", North Carolinians would say, doing what she loves and getting paid to do it.

My other daughters did the same, each one in their field. One is a nurse technician and the other a geography teacher. Jamie my step-daughter decided to be a beautician. All love what they do and get paid for it, and they did it on their own. The work of parents is not to give things to their children, though we give the things that we can, but our job is to plant ideas, give wings to their imagination, to find out the things they have inside, the things they love to do and direct them on how to make a living from that.

Sometimes I picture life as a farm where people are living. Some of the people like to deal with cattle, others with animals; others yet like to cook or to work with dresses etc. Each one grows and learns how to be better at what they like to do. Soon each one is taking positions necessary in the farm, doing what they like and being paid for it.

Modern life is not different. We are born with talents and gifts that make us different one from another. Our first years in life are to discover the things we enjoy. We look around and see grownups that are doing that and making a living. The second step after finding things you like is to learn how to be the best in your field. If you strive to be the best, serve people with your talents and get a little exposure, voilà you will end up doing the things that you like and getting paid for it.

Plant thoughts of joy, choose a path in life that you can be good at and enjoy.. This life is a blessing and we must enjoy the ride. In due time all our thoughts will manifest themselves. Make images of your thoughts, keep the images before you, and declare them. Confess daily the things that you want to be good at. Write your vision. This is our next principle, the power of visualization.

Chapter 8
The Eighth Principle

"Visualization"
The things that you envision are what you get.

In the Old Testament we have the story of Abraham, a man of faith, the friend of God. How his parents had the desire to move from Ur, near Babylon, the cradle of civilization with an intense social life but already requiring a great price to be paid. So they decide to go to another nation "Terah took his son Abram, his grandson Lot son of Haran, and his daughter-in-law Sarai, the wife of his son Abram, and together they set out from Ur of the Chaldeans to go to Canaan. But when they came to Haran, they settled there" (Gen 11:31) It is from Haran that God called Abraham to the new nation, and He promised to make a great nation from his descendants. And then God put an image, a vision, in Abraham's heart.

"Then He (God) brought him (Abraham) outside and said, "Look now toward heaven, and count the stars if you are able to number them." And He said to him, "So shall your descendants be."(Genesis 15:5). Looking at the stars Abraham could see the thousands of descendants he would have.

The image of the stars; when Abraham was shepherding his flocks at the end of the day, he could look at the stars, his vision board, and could see the thousands of descendants he would have, even when he didn't have a son yet.

The power of visualization kept Abraham looking for the future with joy. We all have dreams and things we would like to achieve. Make a board and put on it the images of things you want to reach out. Put the board in a visible location so you can keep looking to the things you want to have. It may be more joy, write JOY on it. If it is a car, choose the model, color and year, be specific. Your thoughts will be focusing on what you are sending to the universe, signals with the desired object you have in mind, the signal, waves, and frequency will resonate with other thoughts and things and they start orchestrating in alignment with your thoughts. It is like a radio transmitter, you are the broadcasting station sending vibrations, waves at say 105 MHz FM, someone has their radio turned in on that frequency and their radio receptor will pick up the incoming wave and resonate on it. In harmony with that wave people will hear your voice and your sound.

Some people may have problems accepting the laws of the

mind, your law of attraction. Say we could go back in history maybe 100 years, and we could say to a group of folks, "hey I can talk in this little box here and someone on the other side of the world will respond to me". People would have said we were madmen, crazy or we were dealing with witchcraft. We could have been stoned. Today radio, TV, and cellular are so common we never think about how "miraculous" they are.

There is coming a day when certain devices will be able to read some of our thoughts. We better start taking control of what we think right now. Texas Instruments just announced, "The Audio is a wireless sensor worn on the neck to capture neurological activity that the brain sends to the vocal cords, and then digitizes this activity using analog and digital technology to turn it into speech".

Artists create things first in their minds, and then they start forming, manifesting their creation. So you, when you visualize the things you want and meditate on them, you are forming your own reality. Abraham saw a multitude when he looked at his son, Isaac. His descendants were about 70 souls when they went to Egypt, and after 400 years there were more than 600,000 men without counting wives, and children under 20 years old. The stars, count the stars if you can. What are your stars? What dreams do you visualize? Have you written them down?

"Write the vision, and make *it* plain on tablets,"(Habakkuk 2:2) Write your vision on tablets, on a board, make it plain. Write a clear, simple vision, an image of the things you want and you are on your way. After you write the vision, or choose the image, start declaring what you see. Declarations of your vision are powerful words that create reality. This is our next principle.

Chapter 9
The Ninth Principle

Declarations, concise confessions that summarize your beliefs.

According to the goals you have, you may design your daily confession, or goals for parts of the day or for special occasions; here you have to deal with your new identity:

I am a new creature predestined for greatness, a child of God fully accepted by the Father. Abundance is God's will for me and I will not settle for less. God is on my side; I will not fear. I am blessed with all spiritual blessings; things are happening for my good even as I speak. I choose not to be offended and I am delivered out of all afflictions and persecutions.

We recommend "Prayers That Avail Much", Word Ministries.

As you have many goals to attain that may pertain to business, personal life, relationships, your way of thinking, etc you may want to prepare and write one declaration for every image you have on your play board.

Say you want a strong marriage and you want to improve your husband-wife relationship. You could say every morning:

Thank you Father for this day, thank you for my spouse, thank you because our marriage grows stronger day by day in the bond of unity because it is founded on Your Word and rooted and grounded in Your love. We decree this day, we have a marriage made in heaven! Father, we thank You for the performance of it, in Jesus' Name.

So you have in your mind the image of a great relationship, in love, in truth, in openness, in respect for one another's opinion, etc. then the image is accompanied with the above declaration. That is your confession about your marriage.

After breakfast you leave home to go to work. As the car warms up you pray for the traffic ahead. You may confess: I am ready to leave home; I declare my trip will be peaceful, everything works for my good. I bless the other drivers. I thank you God for your protection, I speak blessings for everyone in my way. I thank you for the peace and joy that I feel everyday. In Christ name.

You may word it differently every time. The point is to have good thoughts in every stage of the day. That way you are preparing your day, paving it with images and words of grace.

Can we get upset with circumstances we are not expecting? Of course, but that will show that we have gotten out of harmony with our Inner Being. We need to see what thought brought that emotion of anger or sadness. If there is something that we need to do we write down the action we need to take and then let the emotion go. Think about the positive things we have to be thankful for. This way we are back in our good mood and preparing the day for good happenings.

We do not monitor our thoughts but our emotions. Declarations or confession help us to keep focused on the good things we are expecting from life. We must remember this because many times in the past we didn't prepare the day, we took many decisions that brought us to where we are. In order to go where we want, we must design and keep the course of our destination, enjoying the trip. This is our next principle.

Chapter 10
The Tenth Principle

Our way of thinking brought us to the present circumstance, a new way of think will take us far beyond.

It is normal to question "why I am going through circumstances that I didn't ask for". I didn't ask for some of the circumstances I am now living. Well, we reap what we sow. We have received so many wrong ideas and concepts that by default we tend to think, negatively. In order to change the present we have to change our way of thinking. We must accept responsibility for our lives; we can't blame others for the situations we are now in. If someone treated us wrong, our part is that we took it. Going back and blaming people or circumstances does not help. We learn the lessons on the things that happened take the good, trash the bad and pave the future for good and great things.

Paul said "but one thing *I do,* forgetting those things which are behind and reaching forward to those things which are ahead, I press toward the goal for the prize" (Philippians 3:13, 14).

We cannot live in the past. Whatever happened has gone; we learn lessons, shake it off and move on.

Another trapping thought is "what if". That is a nonexistence concept; it is like saying, what if there was no water on the planet!!! Life would not be as it is, if it was possible any how. What if I had married so and so. So what? That is just fantasy; it does not bring any improvement to our lives now. What if I had turned to the right instead of to the left on that street? It is totally a waste of time. So lets get rid of fantasies and let the past stay in the past.

An interesting story we have about Moses before he delivered the people from captivity in Egypt. "Then the LORD said to him, "What is that in your hand?" "A staff," he replied. The LORD said, "Throw it on the ground." Moses threw it on the ground and it became a snake, and he ran from it."(Exodus 4:3,4)

What do you have in your hand; the present, gifts and talents? You have a gift, the present, which is a "present" God gave you, a time given for you to do with it what you want. Throw the staff on the ground and see what God can do. If you feel trapped in a situation, only you can change it, just use whatever you have for good. God is a God of miracles. But He depends on you. He could not use Moses' pilgrim's staff till he released it.

My wife's friend had a terrible accident, in the wreckage she prayed to God to keep her alive; to her amazement she heard the answer of her prayer. "It depends on you". As Christians we are called "God's fellow workers "(I Corinthians 3:9). The Greek uses συνεργοι, sunergoy, ergos = work, sun = together (pronounced sin), from there we have the word synergy, working together. "And we know that all things work together for good to those who love God,"(Romans 8:28)

God's will is for our good. "For I know the thoughts that I think toward you, says the LORD, thoughts of peace and not of evil, to give you a future and a hope. (Jeremiah 29:11. NKJV) We are called to work in synergy with God. He has thoughts of good, now we have to have thoughts of good and then we work together.

My will or God's will? There are some speculations if God's will is specific for each human being. Is it His will that I should be a doctor or a lawyer? And if I choose something else, could I be happy? Is it His will that I should buy apples or oranges? It was His will that someone died at 20 or 60? God gave us the authority to decide what kind of life we want to have. To be an engineer or a singer is your pick. You look inside and see that you are a multi talented person; you choose what makes you happy. Now, we don't know the future and sometimes we are not sure what to choose, then we go to the Lord and present the options. He wants the best for us, we search our soul and we feel the right answer, and we take responsibility for our decisions.

To the young pastor Timothy Paul said ;"For this reason I remind you to fan into flame the gift of God, which is in you through the laying on of my hands." (II Timothy 1:6 NIV). He had the gift inside but he was not sure, Paul ask him to "fan the flame". You have gifts inside of you, discover them. They are your passion. Your passion is your assignment. Be good at it. Work with excellence. Serve people with it. Focus in the joy of doing the things you enjoy. Remember rich and famous people didn't get there because circumstances just fell over their lap. They focused in what they wanted and circumstances and events and people started coming along.

A better life is before us and we are going full force, enjoying the ride, knowing that we have been created to live in joy and abundance. And abundance is for everyone. This is the next principle.

.

Chapter 11
The Eleventh Principle

There is enough for everyone.

This principle solves a lot of anxiety. Many times we are afraid of making a decision about our future because maybe we will not have the provision we need. Other times people don't give because they are afraid they will lack in the future. And others try to get all they can get for the same reason. What if everybody wants to be millionaires, there is not enough for everyone, some may say.

It is said that the earth has the capability to support 40 billion inhabitants if we develop all resources this planet has. Sometime we concentrate in a little space when there are billions of acres not used yet. We look too hard for the place where we live when in fact we are citizens of the world. We live in a global village. We do business across the globe like we do across the street, using the Internet and other technological tools.

Interesting what God told Adam "and God said unto them, Be

fruitful, and multiply, and **replenish** the earth," (Gen 1:28). To replenish or to fill the earth was a command to make the earth a paradise, to take the seed, the cattle and multiply so that humankind would have plenty to live on.

In a competitive world like this some people are worried that there are not enough jobs for everyone, or food, or abundance. But it does not matter where man lives; he always finds a way to overcome any situation. Armed with the right thought he goes for what he wants and his mind brings people, events and situations that help him to live a better life, to overcome.

In the Bible we see how God is the provider. With Him there is no lack. Isaac was living in a time when there was famine in the land but God multiplied his goods one hundredfold. "Then Isaac sowed in that land, and received in the same year a **hundredfold;** and the LORD blessed him." (Gen 26:12)

We believe God established laws in the universe to cooperate with man for his happiness and well being. You plant a crop in the right place and at the right time, you have a harvest. You raise cattle looking for the laws of nature that help them to be strong and reproductive, and you have a great flock. The same laws operate in your mind; you plant seeds of hope, faith, and joy. You study the natural laws of developing a great personality and you reap the fruits.

But above all you know that the Creator is looking after you. He is the God of provision, "And Abraham called the name of the place, The-LORD-Will-**Provide**; as it is said to this day, "In the Mount of the LORD it shall be **provided**." (Gen 22:14).

That's why Paul could say with all assurance "And my God shall supply all your need according to His riches in glory by Christ Jesus." (Philippians 4:19)

For many years I had a suspicion about the "preachers of prosperity". And I know it is easy to promote the "preacher prosperity". But that does not nullify the teaching throughout all the bible about a prosperous life. Abraham was a rich man, so their descendants. To Joshua God said: "Do not let this Book of the Law depart from your mouth; meditate on it day and night, so that you may be careful to do everything written in it. Then you will be prosperous and successful" (Joshua 1:8 NIV).

And to Peter Jesus said:" And everyone who has left houses or brothers or sisters or father or mother or wife or children or lands, for My name's sake, shall receive a hundredfold, and inherit eternal life." (Matthew 19:29). Mark records the same incident in his gospel and he makes sure everyone could understand the hundredfold was to be here, in this life. "who shall not receive a hundredfold now in this time—houses and brothers and sisters and mothers and children and lands, with persecutions—and in the age to come, eternal life." (Mark 10:30).

The problem is not money; the problem is the LOVE of money, greed. But if you ask riches to be a blessing, it is God's will that you prosper. "Beloved, I pray that you may prosper in all things and be in health, just as your soul prospers." (III John 1:2)

The word "prosper" and "prosperity" is referred to in the bible more than one hundred times. But many people have a problem with prosperity. The problem is in their mind. I remember ministering in Brazil in a good church, there were many prosperous members in that church, but for some reason I felt "guilt" for having a car considered to be a "middle class" car. Today I understand my problem. My subconscious mind had been programmed that I was born in a poor family, that I shouldn't "show" prosperity, that would be proud, and God does not accept a "proud" person. I should be humble and poor.

Remember every time we feel guilty or any other negative emotion is because there is a conflict inside. I had to check my thoughts and reprogram my subconscious mind. I had to tell myself that was a lie from the enemy. Dr. I.V. Hilliard says that our subconscious mind is the part of the brain that takes care of repetitious work, habitual patterns. It doesn't know the difference between right or wrong. Whenever our conscious mind tells us and we accept it as a truth, then it starts repeating the pattern.

A classical example is when we are learning to ride a car for first time, we sweat, we keep focused, even the radio is turned off, all attention is on the road and the things that we need to do in order to keep the car moving. But after few training sessions we become more confident. Today we can ride listening to the radio, talking on the phone etc. The subconscious takes care of the habitual chores.

Once the conscience believes something is true then the subconscious accepts it as an habit to be performed. The way to change it is to do the opposite, instructing the conscience about the truthfulness of the new belief.

Yes God has pleasure in our prosperity, ""Let the LORD be magnified, Who has pleasure in the prosperity of His servant" (Psalm 35:27) The prosperity of His people is the prosperity of His kingdom.

Again, all starts in our mind. Keep the positive side of your life always up, no matter what. Be an up lifter, our next principle.

Chapter 12
The Twelfth Principle

Don't go down with people. Be an up lifter.

One of the most important things in life is to keep a joyful mind. We do that by always choosing thoughts that are good, fruitful and positive, that are good for us and at the same time a blessing to others.

In our relationships we want to share our happiness with everyone, but not everyone is ready or willing to receive our way of seeing life. We must remember that there are so many negative thoughts in our world that some people do not believe they can be happy. Everyone is in a different stage in life. Some have an almost sadistic way of thinking, they learn to love suffering. Others have been abused in their childhood. Others had relationships that destroyed their self-esteem. Others want to be happy their way, living for pleasure alone, they replace pleasure for happiness, and so many harm themselves and people around them. Some live in poverty, because they are poor in their thinking, others live in sickness among others reasons, they hate themselves, eat wrong, don't care about life.

Every human being lives in their own stage. Some bring their problems thinking others can solve them, when we are called to solve our own first so we can help others. We may advise, but everyone has to take responsibility for themselves and then make the decisions that are necessary. Some bring so much negative "charge" around them that it can even harm us. We need to approach each person with love, care for them and for ourselves. We cannot let their negativity damage our soul. We must not let their thoughts, by invitation or default become part of us.

The Bible says "Rejoice with those who rejoice, and weep with those who weep." (Rom 12:15). This means, show sympathy with everyone, Greek sym-pathos, walk and feel the same with someone. But sympathy does not mean take their place, live their lives. Christ came to Lazarus' funeral, there "Jesus wept". Then the Jews said, "See how he loved him!" (John 11:35,36). But instead of looking for the cause of their troubles, He brought the solution. Lazarus was brought back to life.

Instead of living someone else troubles, looking for the cause or whom to blame, our approach is looking for solution, working in their mind so they can make productive decisions.

If they are in a mind set that does not allow them to see and to change, our decision should be to show possible direction and let them make their decision. Maybe at this time they are not ready t but the seed was planted and it can bring changes later.

Some organizations tell us that if we have a drug addict that we want to help, we need to let them go to the bottom until they really decide they want to change on their own. If we do not let them go, then we go down with them and we may not be able or will not have the strength to pull them out when they need us. When people are unhappy and they do not want to change their way of thinking, we have to keep ourselves in the positive side no matter what.

When the Bible says "Bear one another's burdens, and so fulfill the law of Christ." in the same context it's says "... each one shall bear his own load." (Galatians 6:2,5).   That means there is a time to help, help with their burden, and there is time to let them go, they are responsible for their own "load".

Some times people have a different and strong point of view and we need to show respect for their point of view. We do not have to agree with someone in order to love them. Christianity has taught us that we should love our enemy. "But I say to you, love your enemies, bless those who curse you, do good to those who hate you, and pray for those who spitefully use you and persecute you," (Matthew 5:43).

We have seen so much hate among men. We never are going to agree with all of someone's point-of-view. We are creatures that develop our own way to see life, and that is the beauty about life. Each one brings to the table their views and from those different views, new ideas, technologies and improvements are created. Any given group can have common grounds and differ on minor points. What keeps the group is the common grounds. If someone does not agree with the common, they have the option to find or create another group that has common grounds with theirs view. And so goes humanity.

Paul said to the Romans: "One person esteems *one* day above another; another esteems every day *alike*. Let each be fully convinced in his own mind." (Romans 14:5). Being convinced in ones own mind doesn't mean to reject the others that do not think alike. Again, we keep together on the common grounds.

One common ground that keeps humanity united is the compassion for our fellow human beings. When there is a catastrophe we see countries that have strong divergent opinions come together to help one in need. To care about the planet and to improve human life are subjects that call us together.

I can have a Muslim friend without agreeing with his ideas or beliefs. He has the right to tell me his beliefs if I want to listen, so vice-versa. If we work together our work is our common ground. If we live in the same neighborhood, the needs of our community are our common ground. We respect one another without agreeing about our beliefs.

I must not compromise my beliefs in order to keep friendship. I respect their opinions and I require they respect my views. We started a Law of Attraction group in my city; we met every other Monday night, with people from all walks of life. We respect and love them all. Our common ground is the improvement of everyone, to help people that want to change their lives in a more productive and abundant way. As a Christian I do not have to agree with everything that is said in the group. But I love them and accept everyone, and it is only through my true love that some can see the light that is inside me. I explain my views and every one of them explain theirs. If anyone sees in me something they would like to have, then they will ask me how to get it, and I will share the gospel of Christ.

Proselytism is the act of forcing people to accept somebody

else point-of-view. Christ didn't come to make proselytes but to make disciples. Disciples are followers because they decide to follow Christ. It is in an atmosphere of love and acceptance that people are attracted. And any true change in life is a question of personal desire and decision.

Being an Up lifter completes the cycle of this teaching. Your dominant thoughts bring about circumstances. Monitoring your feelings make you aware if you are on the right track. You choose joyful thoughts, we walk by faith not by sight or by feelings, so feelings need to be subject to our faith, our belief system, when you "feel" something negative creeping in your mind, you immediately find the source of that feeling, the thought that is bringing the feeling, look at your subconscious mind, tell the real truth to your conscience.

You are thankful for what you have and for what is coming. You ask for the things you need in order to be blessed and to be a blessing. You ask believing you have already received. You allow time between the prayer and the manifestation of it. You rest in the assurance that what you have asked is coming. You visualize and write down whatever you need. You declare to yourself your faith and the confidence that it will come to pass. You do not allow people to interfere in your joy; you are to them a light shining in joy and peace. You have the secret of the kingdom, abundant life. Now you are changing the world, because you have changed yourself.

Epilogue

It is always the light that is in you that will attract people to Christ. The light in you, the Holy Spirit is always working to the renewing of your mind, as we read and grow in the understanding of God's love, grace and abundance, we experience the changing in our lives. We want to be better and we are renewed every morning. The more we think and meditate on those principles, the more we experience a refreshing sense of living, we are blessed and in turn we become a blessing to the ones that want to receive God's blessings.

I believe there are thousands of preachers that have found such principles through the history of the church. We read about Norman V. Peale, Joseph Murphy's "the power of your subconscious mind", and of course, we don't know the names of thousands of them, but through books or especially on the television today we can listen to the preaching of Joel Osteen, Dr. Bill Winston, Fred Price and others that are champions in a biblical positive way of seeing life. Life is a mystery many will say. Where is the truth, if each human being has their own truth? Without going through the semantics and meaning of words, or being too simplistic, we Christians believe that Christ is the Truth, because He "is the mystery of God, namely, Christ, in whom are hidden all the treasures of wisdom and knowledge." (Col. 2:2, 3)

In the Gospel of John He said, "I am the way, the truth, and the life." 14:6, and again "And you shall know the truth, and the truth shall make you free." 8:32, and surely "he who does the truth comes to the light" 3:21, "Everyone who is of the truth hears My voice" 18:37. If we didn't have Jesus Christ we couldn't have the truth. Then every man would have their own "truth" and we would have to try to figure out life on our own. It would all be a question of "opinions".

We believe there is a God; He is an Intelligent Personal God. In love He created the universe, established laws for the good of the creatures He created. He gave them the freedom and intelligence to choose. He saw it and "it was good". Humankind has God's imprint on them, which is our soul. Sin has covered, distorted the image of God in us, which is the cause of so much distress, confusion, negative thoughts and all that is an offspring of sin. But " God, who is rich in mercy, because of His great love with which He loved us, even when we were dead in trespasses, made us alive together with Christ (by grace you have been saved), " (Ephesians 2:4,5) . Yes, God always loved his creatures and in Christ He "has reconciled us to Himself through Jesus Christ, and has given us the ministry of reconciliation" (II Corinthians. 5:18)

Through Jesus' death on the cross we have been reconciled." For it pleased the Father that in Him all the fullness should dwell, and by Him to reconcile all things to Himself, by Him, whether things on earth or things in heaven, having made peace through the blood of His cross. "(Colossians 1:19). And through the cross he nailed our trespasses,"having forgiven you all trespasses, and having wiped out the handwriting of requirements that was against us, which was contrary to us. And He has taken it out of the way, having nailed it to the cross. "(Colossians. 2:13,14)

Now He became the foundation of our life and faith, in Him, Christ the Truth, we build our view of life. "For no one can lay any foundation other than the one already laid, which is Jesus Christ. If any man builds on this foundation using gold, silver, costly stones, wood, hay or straw, his work will be shown " (I Corinthians 3:11-13)

Through meditation and knowledge of the truth centered in Christ and demonstrated in the entire universe we grow in freedom, joy, blessings, maturity. Past mistakes are behind; a renewed life is now and ahead. We can choose good thoughts, dwell in abundant grace, live on trust that there is enough for everyone, He provides for all our needs. We look at problems as opportunities to exercise our faith, our knowledge. We magnify and look for solutions. We are overcomer's, conquerors. Life was meant to be happy, full of contentment, we are expected to bring good circumstance by our thoughts, but if for lack of this knowledge in the past, or for any other reason, we are going through infirmities, loss, or any adverse circumstance, we know now that it was not meant to be like that and we will make the necessary decisions to change that, especially changing the way we think. First of all we put our trust and belief in God, because "With God we will gain the victory, and he will trample down our enemies." (Psalm 108:13). We are made to walk in victory, defeat should never be in our minds, and we read: "But thanks be to God, who gives us the victory through our Lord Jesus Christ." I Corinthians 15:57, and again: "Now thanks be to God who always leads us in triumph in Christ" II Corinthians. 2:14.

We are a work in progress. The ministries we have are for the "perfecting of the saints"(Philippians 4:12), like KJV put it.

Instead of looking at life as a half empty cup we can look at life as a cup that is being filled up till it overflows. We are all designing our own life, perfecting it and building it up. That means, if we didn't get there yet, to the things and feelings and total maturity we want, we are on the way, it's coming. The total perfection we will have in the new heaven and new earth, until then we are all a "work in progress". Now if someone is looking at what is missing, the things that I am not or I don't have, we are attracting more of that in our lives. What we resist persists. So let us look for what we have, let us be thankful for that, let us look for the things that are coming our way, and let us be thankful for that. If it is lacking peace, joy, health, goods etc, do not look for what is missing. Be thankful for what you have, and be thankful for the things that are coming.

Give thanks for your health and more is coming, for your joy, inner peace, provisions, and relationships. Give thanks because more, more and much more is coming. Abundant life starts with the right attitude and the right mind set. You attract what you are. Do not expect God to do for you the things He told us to do. Expect God to do the things He said He will do.

Communion is partnership. Let us do our part, the right mind set, and God will do His.

"I came that they may have life, and have it abundantly. " (John 10:10). The greek for abundant is perissos, meaning "so full that overflows." That is your life.

Biography

I was born in São Paulo Brazil. Early in life we moved back to Pernambuco where I lived with my grandparents. I remember when having rice on Sundays was a feast.

At the age of 10 I went to live with my mom in São Paulo, where I came to know my new born beloved brother Rudi. That was a better life; my step-father was an engineer working with one of the top industries in that country.

In my teens the Lord brought me to Him and 1 year later I went to a bible institute where I could better understand my faith and walking in the Christian life.

By that time we moved to Rio de Janeiro to attend the Seminary and by the 4th year we started our first ministry. After graduation I went to Law School, 5 years, working during the day and having evening classes.

We started practicing law in the family court and at the same time we were teaching Greek and NT in the seminary. By that time we were the vice superintendent of the local High School, a minister of a 400 member church and working in the denomination as the president of the churches association.

In the 90's we came back to São Paulo, the city of Taubaté to assume a new ministry and then to teach at the local University. All that running drained my spiritual energy and finally took a toll on my marriage and ministry.

In 1993 I came to the USA, to the peaceful city of Burlington NC. It was a new start, a second change. "If we are faithless, He remains faithful; He cannot deny Himself." II Timothy 2:13 Here I had the blessing to know Nancy my wife, and with her we started a new path, a new life.

10 year ago I opened "Lacerda Realty Inc". The Lord has blessed us, through the company we can buy and build some houses here and in Brazil. God gave me the privilege to visit Jerusalem and Israel. We went to Greece; we also visited Ephesus and other countries.

Above all I am so thankful for my Lord and Savior Jesus Christ for restoring me and letting me have the privilege of preaching in many churches, to minister and to grow in the knowledge of His Amazing Grace.

Today I am living the best days of my life because living and having the understanding of the principles exposed here make life a feast everyday. Christ came to bring Heaven to Earth and living in His kingdom life is heaven.

"The Kingdom of Heaven is among you".

Bibliography

God. The Bible. New King James Version, wherever another version is not mentioned.

Dr. I.V. Hilliard. Mental Toughness for Success" . Light Publications. 2003

Dr. Bill Wilson " The Renewing of the Mind". Living Word Center. Chicago. Tape Series

Lynne McTaggart. "The Field". Harper Perennial. 2001

John Piper. "Desiring God". Multnomah Books. 1996

Rick Warren. "The Purpose Driven Life". Zondervan. 2002

Bill Bryson. "A Short History of Nearly Everything". Broadway Books. NY. 2004

Dr. C. Thomas Anderson. "Becoming a Millionaire God's Way". Faith Words. 2006

Dave Ramsey. "Financial Peace". Viking. 2003.

Joel Osteen. "Your Best Life Now". Warner Faith.2004.

Stephen R. Covey. The 7 Habits of Highly Effective People". A Fireside Book. 1989.

Rick Pitino. "Success is a Choice". Broadway Books. 1997.

Liddel and Scott. "An Intermediate Greek-English Lexicon". Oxford. 30th Edition.

Dr. Wayne Dyers. "10 Secrets for Success and Inner Peace".

Hay House. 2001

Gloria Copeland. "God's Will is Prosperity". KCP. Texas. 1991.

John C. Maxwell. "Thinking for a Chance. 11 Ways highly Successful People Approach Life and Work". Warner Books. 2003

David J. Schwartz. "The Magic of Thinking Big".Fireside. 1987

Robert T. Kiyosaki. "Rich Dad, Poor Dad". Warner Books. 2001

Myles Monroe. "Kingdom Principles".Destiny. Bahamas.2006

      "   " The Most Important Person on Earth".2007.

Made in the USA